# It Just Occurred to Me...